FAVE CHAMPIONSHIP PLAYER: ....
....

FAVE SCOTTISH PREMIERSHIP PLAYER: ....
....

BEST GOAL SCORED IN UK LEAGUES: ....
....

I WANT .... TO WIN THE PREMIER LEAGUE!

I WANT ....TO WIN THE SCOTTISH PREMIERSHIP!

I WANT .... TO WIN THE CHAMPIONSHIP!

THE TOP SCORER IN UK LEAGUES WILL BE: ....
....

It's goal o'clock, guys!

These quick-fire facts and stats will boost your Premier League brainpower. It's the most exciting history lesson you'll ever have!

PREMIER POWER!

WHAT IS IT?

The Premier League is the highest level of the four professional football leagues in England. It is made up of 20 clubs, and teams from Wales may compete. It's one of the most exciting sports competitions in the world – its thrilling mix of fantastic footy stars, silky skills and famous clubs means that you'll never want to miss a minute of the action!

HOW DOES IT WORK?

Between August and May, each team plays each other at home and away. The club with the most points at the end of the season wins the Premier League trophy. Simple! The top four teams qualify for the following season's Champions League. The bottom three teams are relegated to the Championship.

WHEN DID IT BEGIN?

The Premier League first kicked off on 15 August, 1992 – before heroes like Harry Kane and Paul Pogba were even born! Sheffield United striker Brian Deane scored the first goal and Manchester United were the first Premier League champions. Spurs' Teddy Sheringham won the first Golden Boot award with 22 goals.

MY UK TEAMS & PLAYERS BOOK!

This book is packed with facts, stats and puzzles all about the top teams and players in the UK. You'll discover loads of awesome info about the Premier League's biggest stars, plus heroes from the past. On these pages you can write your footy dreams and details.

MY NAME: ....

AGE: ....

CITY/TOWN: ....

MY TOP THREE UK TEAMS:

1 ....

2 ....

3 ....

BEST EVER PLAYER IN THE UK: ....

....

BEST EVER TEAM IN THE UK: ....

....

BEST EVER MANAGER IN THE UK: ....

....

FAVE PREMIER LEAGUE PLAYER: ....

....

You gotta pick Pogba!

Suuuuper Alan Shearer!

WHY IS IT SO AMAZING?

Goals, talented players, huge transfers, great games... there are loads of reasons why fans love the Premier League! Every weekend there's a mega meeting between teams going for the title or relegation rivals desperate for three points. It's incredible to watch in the stadiums or on TV. If you support a big club like Manchester City, Manchester United, Spurs or Arsenal, or a smaller team trying to cause an upset, you can't take your eyes off the pitch.

STAT ATTACK

MOST PREMIER LEAGUE TITLES: Manchester United (13)

MANAGER WITH MOST TITLES: Sir Alex Ferguson, Manchester United (13)

MOST PREMIER LEAGUE GOALS: Alan Shearer (260)

TEAMS THAT HAVE WON THE TITLE: Manchester United, Blackburn Rovers, Arsenal, Chelsea, Manchester City, Leicester City

TEAMS THAT HAVE PLAYED IN EVERY SEASON: Arsenal, Chelsea, Everton, Liverpool FC, Manchester United, Tottenham Hotspur

CHAMPIONSHIP CLOSE-UP!

The second-highest football league, the EFL Championship is a classy competition guaranteed to deliver fun, thrills, plus the joy of promotion and the fear of relegation. Jump into these fast facts...

WHAT IS IT?

The EFL Championship is the league below the Premier League. It has 24 teams, with every club's ultimate goal being to win promotion to the Premier League. With more games than the Premier League, it's bursting with big-match meetings every weekend. It also has the added excitement of the play-offs and the heartache of relegation. The action never stops!

Ladies and gents, cheer on the Championship stars!

HOW DOES IT WORK?

The teams that finish first and second are promoted to the Premier League for the following season. Coming between third and sixth means you have the chance to win the play-offs and become the third team to reach the Premier League. The bottom three clubs drop down to join League 1. There's usually something to play for in every Championship game!

WHEN DID IT BEGIN?

When the dinosaurs were around. OK, not that long ago, but the Championship was part of the Football League set up way back in 1888. It became the Championship in 2004 and since then, big clubs like Leicester City, Newcastle United, Aston Villa, Norwich City, Southampton, West Ham United and Sunderland have all been part of the league's famous history.

WHY IS IT SO AMAZING?

The Championship doesn't have the superstars and mega-rich clubs of the Premier League, but for excitement and entertainment it's one of the best leagues in Europe. There are big attendances in cities like Sheffield, Leeds, Birmingham, Derby and Nottingham and every team wants the glory of reaching the Premier League. It's tough, tense and totally nail-biting!

STAT ATTACK

MOST TITLES: Leicester City & Manchester City (7)

LONGEST CURRENT CHAMPIONSHIP STAY: Ipswich Town (since 2002)

TOP SEASON SCORER (SINCE 2004): Glenn Murray, Crystal Palace, 30 goals

MOST POINTS IN A SEASON (SINCE 2004): Reading, 106

Save this pen. keeper!

The slick footy in Scotland goes under the microscope now. Get ready for some stats, facts and fun stuff all about the Scottish Premiership.

SCOTTISH SPOTLIGHT!

WHAT IS IT?

The Scottish Premiership is Scotland's biggest competition. Top-division football has been played in the country since the 1890s and the Scottish Premiership was created in 2013. Between 1998 and 2013 it was called the Scottish Premier League (SPL). Glasgow, Aberdeen, Dundee, Edinburgh and Motherwell are some of the cities and towns whose clubs have a famous history in the competition.

Between May 2016 and December 2017, **Celtic** went a record **56** Premiership games without defeat. They didn't lose for **69** games in Scottish league and cup games during that time.

HOW DOES IT WORK?

The Premiership has 12 teams. Each team plays each other three times, in a mix of one or two home and away games, to make 33 games. The league then splits into the top and bottom six. Each team in each split plays the other five teams once. The bottom team is relegated to the Scottish Championship and the 11th-placed club plays off with the Championship runners-up for a spot in the Premiership.

WHEN DID IT BEGIN?

The Scottish Premiership first got its name in 2013. In the SPL's first two seasons, between 1998 and 2000, the league had just ten teams. The split after 33 games first came into play in 2001, so Scottish fans are well used to the system now – it's not as complicated as it sounds! Only the top team in the Premiership has the chance to reach the Champions League!

WHY IS IT SO AMAZING?

It's a famous footy league with plenty of traditional clubs and very passionate supporters. Celtic and Rangers, from Glasgow, are the biggest Premiership teams with huge stadiums and the best squads. The split system is different to pro leagues in England and creates a lot of excitement at the end of the season. It's a small league compared to others, but is still watched by millions of fans around the world.

STAT ATTACK

MOST SCOTTISH TITLES (OVERALL): Rangers (54)
MOST TITLES IN A ROW: Rangers and Celtic (9)
MOST TOP DIVISION GOALS: Jimmy McGrory (410)
MOST SEASONS IN TOP DIVISION: Celtic (1890–present)

CAPTAIN CLUES!

Can you name the captains of these Premier League clubs? If you need some help, there's a cheeky clue with each picture.

1 His name rhymes with Larry Paybill!
2 Big pals with Hazard and Lukaku!
3 Likes to drive a 'Jag'!
4 His name's a sunny place in Spain!
5 Makes his Mark for The Hammers!
6 Also played for Sunderland and England!
7 He's a Fox in his own box!
8 Simon says, 'Defend the ball!'

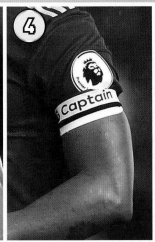

1 ANSWER ....
2 ANSWER ....
3 ANSWER ....
4 ANSWER ....

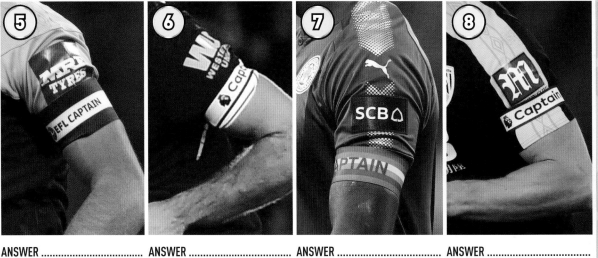

5 ANSWER ....
6 ANSWER ....
7 ANSWER ....
8 ANSWER ....

ANSWERS ON PAGE 94.

MOHAMED SALAH

ALL ABOUT
MANCHESTER CITY

One of the biggest clubs in the world, Manchester City have a superstar team, a mega manager and a trophy cabinet full of silverware!

GAME PLAN

When manager Pep Guardiola took charge in 2016, Manchester City began playing an attacking style of football. The players like to win the ball quickly and set up quick counter attacks, but they are also happy to play lots of passes and pick the right moment to move forwards and shoot at goal. The Citizens are probably the League's most entertaining team to watch.

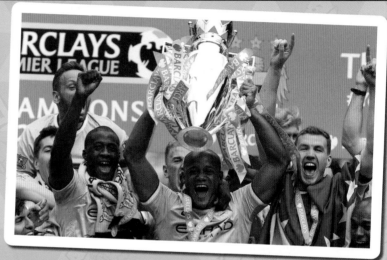

TROPHY TALK

Manchester City have won loads of trophies in the last few years, landing the Premier League title in 2018, 2014 and 2012. They have also won the FA Cup and League Cup (twice) this decade. Ever since the club was bought by Abu Dhabi United Group in 2008 they have signed some of the world's best players and competed for glory in the Champions League every season since 2011.

STARS TO WATCH...

EDERSON
GOALKEEPER
Commanding & agile

SERGIO AGUERO
FORWARD
Explosive in front of goal

RAHEEM STERLING
MIDFIELDER
Quick, cool & skilful

KEVIN DE BRUYNE
MIDFIELDER
Top passer & goalscorer

NICKNAME: The Citizens
STADIUM: Etihad Stadium
CAPACITY: 55,017
HOME KIT: Sky blue shirts & white shorts
YEAR FOUNDED: 1880
CLUB LEGENDS: Colin Bell, Mike Summerbee, Francis Lee, Bert Trautmann, Georgi Kinkladze

PLAYER POWER

Manchester City have spent hundreds of millions to buy global superstars, like Sergio Aguero, Kevin De Bruyne, Raheem Sterling and Bernardo Silva. Experienced heroes Vincent Kompany, David Silva and Yaya Toure were vital in their championship victories while John Stones, Kyle Walker and Aymeric Laporte form a brilliant defence.

Call us the best Prem team ever!

Manchester City beat fierce rivals Manchester United 6-1 in 2011. United were the reigning champions at the time too!

BIG BUY: Aymeric Laporte (£57m in 2018) **BARGAIN BUY:** Vincent Kompany (£6m in 2008) **CAPTAIN:** Vincent Kompany
TOP SCORER: Sergio Aguero (190+) **FAMOUS WIN:** v QPR in 2012 to win first Premier League title

SCORING WITH STYLE!

Watching Manchester City turn on the style is one of the best sights in footy! Here are five reasons why they <u>rock</u> the Premier League and Europe.

Score ten goals every game, please!

GREAT GUARDIOLA

When he was the manager at Barcelona and Bayern Munich, Pep Guardiola won 21 major trophies. These included six league titles, two Champions Leagues and three FIFA Club World Cups. The Spaniard gets his teams to play with speed and slick skills and he's used to winning leagues and cups every year – Pep's the reason Manchester City are so far ahead of Chelsea, Liverpool FC, Manchester United and the rest of the best!

TEENAGE TALENT

Manchester City are not just about multi-million transfers. Their Etihad Campus, which is right next to the main Etihad Stadium, has 17 training pitches, a 7,000-seater academy stadium and can take around 400 academy players. Brahim Diaz and Phil Foden are two top teenagers to have reached The Citizen's first team recently to play alongside big stars like Sergio Aguero and Kevin De Bruyne.

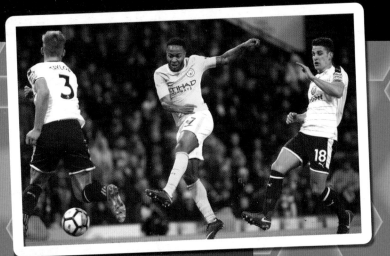

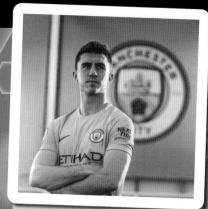

TOP TRANSFERS

Any player in the world would want to pull on the sky-blue Manchester City shirt and show off their skills at the Etihad Stadium. City can attract and spend the cash on super signings every year. Defenders Kyle Walker and Aymeric Laporte cost more than £100 million in total and Bernando Silva, Ederson and Benjamin Mendy are £130 million worth of top new players bought last season.

GOALS GALORE

Manchester City were the Premier League's top scorers when they won the title in 2018. By Christmas of that season they had smashed in 60 league goals, scoring over 100 in the competition during 2017. They became the first team to bag at least five goals in three Premier League games in a row and beat title rivals Liverpool FC 5–0 and Tottenham Hotspur 4–1.

CHAMPIONSHIP CHASERS

Whether it's with Pep Guardiola or previous managers Manuel Pellegrini and Roberto Mancini, Manchester City have become regular winners of the Premier League. Since 2011 they have three titles, with two runners-up spots. The Manchester City Women's team has also picked up silverware, including the Women's Super League and FA Women's Cup. The club's trophy cabinet is massive!

In 2017 **The Citizens** scored seven Premier League goals in one game for only the second time. They beat Stoke City **7–2**, but in 2013 they stuffed Norwich City **7–0**!

ALL ABOUT CHELSEA

Chelsea fans are used to seeing their club win championships and cups. Take a look at their team, tactics and impressive trophy count!

GAME PLAN

When Chelsea stormed to the title in 2017, they did so with a rock-solid back three and wing-backs who linked up fantastically with the midfield and attack. The Blues have special talents in the centre of the pitch, including playmakers Eden Hazard and Cesc Fabregas, as well as a box-to-box hero in N'Golo Kante. Super subs like Pedro and Willian can turn games after coming off the bench.

TROPHY TALK

After Manchester United, Chelsea are the most successful team in the Premier League. They won the trophy five times between 2005 and 2017 under managers Jose Mourinho, Carlo Ancelotti and Antonio Conte. The Blues have also lifted every other major honour, including the FA Cup, League Cup, Champions League and Europa League.

STARS TO WATCH...

EDEN HAZARD
MIDFIELDER
Super skills & dribbling

N'GOLO KANTE
MIDFIELDER
Perfect tackling & passing

MARCOS ALONSO
DEFENDER
Awesome free-kicks

ALVARO MORATA
STRIKER
Classy finisher in the box

NICKNAME: The Blues
STADIUM: Stamford Bridge
CAPACITY: 41,631
HOME KIT: Blue shirt & shorts
YEAR FOUNDED: 1905
CLUB LEGENDS: John Terry, Frank Lampard, Gianfranco Zola, Peter Osgood, Ron Harris

PLAYER POWER

Chelsea have a strong core of players, with goalkeeper Thibaut Courtois, centre-back Gary Cahill and midfielder Eden Hazard the first names on the team sheet. Victor Moses and Marcos Alonso take the wing-back spots and Danny Drinkwater, Ross Barkley, Willian and Alvaro Morata bring attacking options. In defence, Antonio Rudiger and Andreas Christensen have slotted in very well.

In **2017 Chelsea** became the first team to win **30** Premier League games in a single season.

BIG BUY: Alvaro Morata (**£60m** in 2017) **BARGAIN BUY:** Victor Moses (**£9m** in 2012) **CAPTAIN:** Gary Cahill
BIGGEST PREM WIN: 8–0 v Wigan (2010) **FAMOUS WIN:** v Bayern Munich in **2012** Champions League Final

BRILLIANT BLUES!

What are the secrets behind Chelsea's success? Here are five reasons why The Blues are a Premier League mega club!

AWESOME ABRAMOVICH

The man who has helped make the Blues brilliant in the 21st century is Roman Abramovich. The Russian billionaire bought Chelsea in 2003 and turned them into title challengers and a force in the Champions League by buying world-class players and hiring superb managers like Antonio Conte, Jose Mourinho and Carlo Ancelotti. Abramovich also transformed Chelsea's training ground into a top-class facility.

CAPITAL GAINS

Tottenham Hotspur, Arsenal and West Ham United are among London's leading Premier League clubs, but Chelsea have probably been the capital's best team over the last 20 years. They've won 20 important trophies in that time, compared to Arsenal's 17. Between 2003 and 2017 The Blues only finished outside of the top four once – fantastic form!

SLICK STADIUM

Stamford Bridge currently holds about 41,000 fans, which is much lower than Manchester United, Arsenal and Spurs' grounds. In the 2020s, Chelsea plan to redevelop it into one of the best stadiums in the world, with a capacity of approximately 60,000. The development could cost about £1 billion, but would give Chelsea even more power to win trophies and attract the best stars to Stamford Bridge.

SURPRISE STARS

Chelsea seem to have a special knack for bringing in new surprise players, who quickly become fans' favourites! Centre-back Cesar Azpilicueta wasn't a well-known player before he arrived at Stamford Bridge, but he's now a double title-winner and vital in defence. Marcos Alonso, Andreas Christensen, Antonio Rudiger and Davide Zappacosta have all become important first-teamers since joining The Blues' squad in recent years.

In the first **25** League games in 2017–18, **Alonso** scored an impressive **six** goals.

TEAM LEADERS

Chelsea's recent teams have been packed with strong leaders and winning characters. Former captain John Terry was a huge influence between 2000 and 2017, backed up by legends like Frank Lampard, Didier Drogba and Michael Essien. Current skipper Gary Cahill bosses the pitch and Kante, Fabregas, Azpilicueta and David Luiz are all leaders in the team.

HAIR WE GO!

These Premier League stars have had a proper mix-up at the barbers! Work out which hairstyle should go with which player...

1. David Silva, Manchester City
2. David De Gea, Manchester United
3. Theo Walcott, Everton

d

4. Alexis Sanchez, Manchester United
5. Kasper Schmeichel, Leicester City
6. Willian, Chelsea

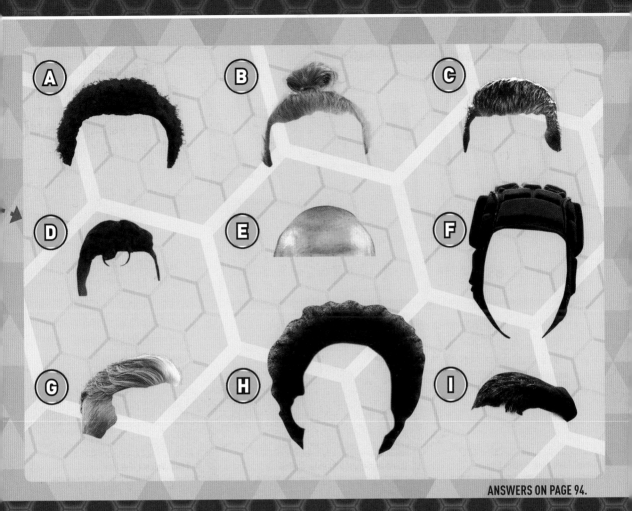

ANSWERS ON PAGE 94.

Dele Alli, Tottenham Hotspur

Andy Carroll, West Ham United

Petr Cech, Arsenal

TOP 20

PREMIER LEAGUE SUPERSTARS

Here's the ultimate rundown of the Premier League's best players, including goal heroes, magical midfielders and indestructible defenders. Discover who'll make it to the No.1 spot...

19

WAYNE ROONEY

EVERTON FORWARD

Rooney's a total Premier League legend! Since he was 16, he's banged in wonder goals and ripped defenders apart with his smart skills and boxer-like strength. He's still running the show back at his boyhood club, Everton, and scored one of the goals of the season with a stunner from his own half against West Ham United.

ROBERTO FIRMINO

LIVERPOOL FC STRIKER

The brilliant Brazil star took a while to find his goalscoring boots at Liverpool FC. Linking up with Salah and Sane in attack, Firmino's since become a quality No.9 who can burn past the opposition and also pop up in the box to tuck away a chance. He's very entertaining on the pitch and The Reds' fans think rockin' Robbie is ace!

Kante made **379** tackles in his first **95** league games.

20

18

N'GOLO KANTE

CHELSEA MIDFIELDER

Kante doesn't blast goals every week or pull out eye-popping tricks, but he's a vital part of Chelsea's Premier League and Champions League dream. The France midfielder has the energy, power, vision, speed and footy brain to win the ball and get his team on the attack. Back-to-back Premier League winners' medals proves Kante's a class act.

DELE ALLI

TOTTENHAM HOTSPUR MIDFIELDER

Spurs have a special talent in the shape of this goalscoring and goal-creating midfielder. The England hero has fantastic footwork and loves to ping a pass to Kane or Eriksen, or dribble into the box and beat the keeper. From Alli's first 93 Premier League games he scored 33 and made 23 assists. Very, very special.

17

JAMIE VARDY

16

LEICESTER CITY STRIKER

Speed, skill, strength, accuracy, cool head – just some of the words to describe this Premier League hero! Vardy blasted Leicester City to the title in 2016, scoring 24 goals and has reached double figures in his last three seasons. He's the perfect striker for counter-attacking footy and never gives defenders a second to rest.

JOHN STONES

MANCHESTER CITY CENTRE-BACK

Manchester City paid Everton £47 million for Stones, but that was cash well spent as the England star's now one of the world's most complete defenders. Partnering Kompany, or Otamendi in the backline, he can coolly pass the ball out but also has the power to tackle and block danger. A hero of Manchester City's 2018 title-winning team.

15

VIRGIL VAN DIJK

LIVERPOOL FC CENTRE-BACK

Another giant defender with a giant price tag, the Reds paid a record £75 million to Southampton for Van Dijk in 2018. The Dutchman cost top money because he's a commanding centre-back who uses his speed, control, heading and well-timed tackles to keep the ball well away from the Reds' goal.

14

> Arrrr! I make screamin' saves!

De Gea joined United from Atletico for **£18.9** million a then British record for a keeper in 2011.

13

DAVID DE GEA

MANCHESTER UNITED GOALKEEPER

With Premier League, Europa League, FA Cup and League Cup medals, De Gea's already a big fave with the Old Trafford fans. He's been the best keeper in the country for years and pulls out superhero saves every week. When he's wearing Spain's No.1 shirt De Gea also proves why he's so highly rated.

MESUT OZIL

ARSENAL MIDFIELDER

One of the best bits of transfer business in 2018 was when Arsenal saw Ozil sign a new three-year deal to remain a Gunner. The German's a genius with the ball and in five years at the club he created around 50 Premier League goals. Ozil's the perfect player to join midfield and attack and has pin-point passing and free-kicks.

12

10

CESC FABREGAS

CHELSEA MIDFIELDER

The little Spain midfielder first impressed Premier League fans as a 16 year-old with Arsenal and is still only in his early 30s. The playmaker bosses games thanks to his laser-guided passing and has two League medals with Chelsea. Stopping fabulous Fabregas from doing his stuff is very difficult!

Pogba first joined United aged **16**, then left when he was **19** before re-joining from Juventus at **23**.

11

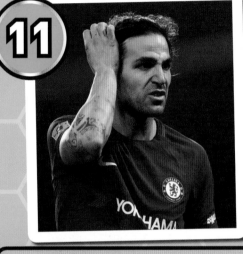

PAUL POGBA

MANCHESTER UNITED MIDFIELDER

Powerful Pogba has the weapons to control any game – he's so big, strong and quick that other teams run and hide! The France star is a box-to-box midfielder but is most dangerous when he's bursting into the opposition's half and setting up his forwards. Fierce free-kicks and long-range strikes are also part of his game plan.

RAHEEM STERLING

MANCHESTER CITY MIDFIELDER

In 2017–18, Sterling enjoyed his best ever season, reaching double figures for League goals for the first time and picking up his first Premier League medal. He can play anywhere in attack and frightens defenders with his pace. England's pint-sized hero also scored his first headed goal in two years!

9

8

DAVID SILVA

MANCHESTER CITY MIDFIELDER

Watching David Silva flick, pass and ping the ball around a Premier League pitch for 90 minutes is a master class in midfield magic! The Spaniard's left foot is capable of anything and his playing style alongside Fernandinho, Sane and De Bruyne also shows what a team player he is. Silky Silva's worth his weight in gold!

Salah is so good he even has his own song!

I'm goal crazy!

7

6

PIERRE-EMERICK AUBAMEYANG

ARSENAL STRIKER

When Alexis Sanchez left for Manchester United, the goal machine Arsenal replaced him with was £60-million star shooter Aubameyang. He'd scored over 100 times for Dortmund and with his speed, close control and ability to find space in the box, Arsenal fans have another goal king to worship.

MOHAMED SALAH

LIVERPOOL FC FORWARD

After a quiet spell with Chelsea between 2014 to 2015, Mo Salah rejoined the Premier League from Roma in 2017 to become an instant hit at Liverpool FC. The fleet-footed forward struck over 30 goals in his debut season as a Red and showed off a deadly mix of speed, tricks, dribbling and shooting accuracy.

Sanchez also scored **47** in **141** games for Barcelona.

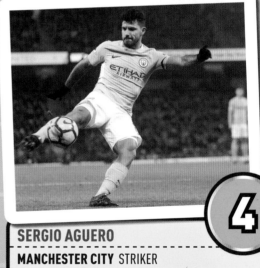

5

4

ALEXIS SANCHEZ

MANCHESTER UNITED FORWARD

Ronaldo, Beckham and Cantona have all worn Manchester United's famous No.7 shirt. Sanchez is another legend that will wear it with pride. The Chile forward is hot stuff in front of goal and is a major threat picking the ball up on the wing to set up attacks for The Red Devils.

SERGIO AGUERO

MANCHESTER CITY STRIKER

With 143 goals in just 203 Premier League games, it's easy to see why Aguero's the most feared Manchester City striker ever! The Argentina star now has three championship medals and can lead the attack as a lone frontman or link up with Gabriel Jesus in a deadly double act. Aguero's sharp movement and quick-fire shooting creates lots of chances for Pep Guardiola's team.

3

Thumbs up for my slick skills!

EDEN HAZARD

CHELSEA MIDFIELDER

One of Chelsea's all-time top players, Hazard needs just a tiny bit of space and he'll create a chance and set The Blues on the attack. The Belgium playmaker can play in the middle or out wide, is a master dribbler and very difficult to knock off the ball. On average in the Premier League Hazard scores once every three games, an impressive stat for a midfielder.

In **93** Prem games De Bruyne had created **42** goal assists.

2

KEVIN DE BRUYNE

MANCHESTER CITY MIDFIELDER

Like Salah, De Bruyne never had a chance to shine at Chelsea but in sky blue he's been phenomenal. Not only is Kev very skilful with powerful shooting and a great passing range, but he works hard for the team and makes tackles to win the ball back. He's a Manchester City legend and vital as the club plans to conquer the Premier and Champions Leagues for years to come.

NO.1 SUPERSTAR

I'm the No.1! What a result!

In **2018** **Kane** became the third player to score over **20 goals** in the **Premier League** for **four seasons** in a row.

1

HARRY KANE

TOTTENHAM HOTSPUR STRIKER

'King Kane' rules for Spurs! Harry's an absolute goal grabber, hitting 100 in just 141 Premier League games and already has a stack of golden boot trophies. He's so tough to stop because he can power past defenders or turn with the ball and hit the target from distance. Hat-tricks, headers, penalties, screamers – Kane can do anything and is the No.1 player in the Premier League because of it!

Topps MATCH ATTAX

PLAY TO WIN!

As every football manager knows, you need strategy as well as top players to be a winner. Here are five top tips to help you collect and play like a pro. You'll soon be a Match Attax master!

I'm a hat-trick hero!

100 Club

101

101

1 101 – THE ULTIMATE MATCH ATTAX CARD

Look out for the new 101-rated card in packets. The 101-er is unbeatable so it's a no-brainer to get one into your line-up!

2 AWAY KITS AND HAT-TRICK HEROES!

Away Kit cards feature players in their team's alternative strip and are a must-have for your team. These cool cards could score you two goals meaning playing from home need never be a problem again. Also don't miss out on Hat-Trick Heroes, exclusively available in Match Attax Extra, featuring players who've scored trebles throughout the season. They could score you three goals!

3 SUPER SUBS!

Each team has 11 players and 3 subs so if you want to switch things up, you'll need a good impact player coming off the bench. You can surprise an opponent and turn the game into your favour with a well-timed sub!

NEW MATCH ATTAX APP!

4 TALKING TACTICS

Change the game with Tactic cards. These super collectable game-changers include injury, referee and agent cards. They can damage an opponent's score, increase your transfer budget, make an opponent swap their player and even boost your cards. You're allowed to use two of them in each match so get them into your squad to take the win!

Let's go. it's time to up the game!

5 ATTACKING DEFENDERS, DEFENSIVE ATTACKERS!

Look out for players who are good in attack and defence, mainly all-rounder midfielders and flying full-backs like Paul Pogba and Marcos Alonso! These guys can spring a shock on an opponent out of nowhere!

You can now get the new Match Attax app to collect, swap and play with thousands of other fans! All you need to do is:

STEP 1. Search PL Match Attax on your App store.

STEP 2. Download the new Match Attax App.

STEP 3. Scan codes found in Match Attax packets to get free digital cards.

STEP 4. Build your digital team and join the fun!

Download on the **App Store**　GET IT ON **Google Play**

SWAP & PLAY TOUR

If you want to find out more about Match Attax, come along to one of our Swap & Play Tour events! You'll be able to swap cards to complete your collection, play games against other collectors and even take part in the Match Attax World Championships!

For more information about dates and events go to **toppsfootball.com**

SPOT THE STARS!

Keep your eyes peeled!

These 15 footy heroes rocked the Championship in 2017–2018. Can you find them all in the grid?

```
B  M  W  F  S  Q  W  V  O  E  W  H
Y  Y  Y  A  A  V  E  T  J  C  V  V
N  L  C  I  V  R  O  O  F  E  B  V
X  O  Z  V  I  K  X  K  U  G  K  B
A  G  N  O  L  A  B  M  O  S  S  A
R  R  F  G  L  T  D  N  J  I  N  I
R  E  Z  Y  E  A  O  S  Q  N  X  X
Q  I  N  R  V  S  Q  N  V  I  L  T
F  D  A  I  I  L  S  H  C  T  W  O
G  R  E  D  D  Z  U  E  D  A  S  G
H  S  D  Z  G  A  K  Q  S  N  R  F
W  A  K  H  A  D  M  W  A  O  W  T
M  I  J  B  O  V  R  Q  R  B  A  C
G  Y  M  O  Z  I  O  C  D  D  O  N
F  A  W  H  T  S  L  P  Y  C  X  J
B  Q  I  L  N  A  C  E  V  C  T  X
W  A  T  K  I  N  S  E  T  U  I  M
E  K  R  A  L  C  R  P  A  T  Z  U
```

- BONATINI
- DAVIES
- VYDRA
- CLARKE
- JOTA
- WATKINS
- BAMBA
- MADINE
- ROOFE
- ASSOMBALONGA
- HOILETT
- SESSEGNON
- MADDISON
- REID
- SAVILLE

ANSWERS ON PAGE 94.

PIERRE-EMERICK AUBAMEYANG

ALL ABOUT
MANCHESTER UNITED

They haven't won the League since 2013, but Manchester United still have more trophies in their cabinet than most clubs can even dream of!

TROPHY TALK

Manchester United are the most successful Premier League team ever! They won the first title back in 1993 and picked up the trophy a further 12 times over the next 20 years.

As well as a stack of League crowns, The Red Devils collected 12 FA Cup wins up to 2016, plus five League Cups and three European Cups and Champions Leagues. They're such a massive club that if they don't win a trophy every season, it's a shock!

GAME PLAN

With over 70,000 fans behind them at Old Trafford, Manchester United like to entertain and play fast, counter-attacking footy. Boss Jose Mourinho also builds a solid defence, but United play with attacking full-backs and their wide players bomb into the box as much as possible. Midfielders like Paul Pogba, Juan Mata and Nemanja Matic are all capable of magical touches and passes.

STARS TO WATCH...

ALEXIS SANCHEZ
STRIKER
Dangerous around the box

DAVID DE GEA
GOALKEEPER
Acrobatic & strong

PHIL JONES
CENTRE-BACK
Powerful tackling & heading

MARCUS RASHFORD
FORWARD
Speedy on the wings

NICKNAME: The Red Devils
STADIUM: Old Trafford
CAPACITY: 74,994
HOME KIT: Red shirt & white shorts
YEAR FOUNDED: 1878
CLUB LEGENDS: George Best, David Beckham, Cristiano Ronaldo, Ryan Giggs

PLAYER POWER

The Manchester United team is always packed with some of footy's biggest stars. Jesse Lindgard and Marcus Rashford are academy lads that have burst into the first team, and expensive heroes like Romelu Lukaku (£75m) and Nemanja Matic (£40m) bring goals, power and big-game experience. De Gea is one of the best keepers on the planet and new hero Alexis Sanchez is a special talent in attack.

Manchester United are the only team to have scored over **1,900** goals in the Premier League.

Piggyback to the dressing room!

BIG BUY: Paul Pogba (**£89m** in 2016) **BARGAIN BUY:** Chris Smalling (**£10m** in 2010) **TEEN STAR:** Angel Gomes
BIGGEST PREMIER LEAGUE WIN: 9-0 v Ipswich (1995) **FAMOUS WIN:** v Chelsea in **2008** Champions League Final

RED DEVILS ROCK!

With a talented team, top manager and hugely impressive history, it's no surprise why Manchester United are chasing trophies every season. Take a closer look at the club...

FERGIE FLIES HIGH

The person Manchester United can thank for their 13 League crowns since 1993 is former manager Sir Alex Ferguson. He won all those titles between 1993 and 2013, managing over 800 Premier League games and more than 1,400 in all competitions. Ferguson won a staggering 528 of his 810 Premier League games and bagged over 30 trophies with Manchester United.

SANCHEZ THE SUPER SEVEN

You'll read about other famous Manchester United No.7s in this book, and Alexis Sanchez is the latest to grace the shirt. Wearing this number for the Old Trafford club means you must have bags of talent, passion and skill to light up the crowd. Sanchez joined the Red Devils in January 2018 after three and a half years at Arsenal, where he scored 60 Premier League goals in just 122 games.

HOMEGROWN HEROES

The Red Devils have a proud history of always having at least one homegrown player in their first team squad since October 1937. Stretching back to over 3,900 games, the current squad has academy heroes like Jesse Lingard, Marcus Rashford, Paul Pogba and Joel Pereira. In the past David Beckham, Paul Scholes, Danny Welbeck and Jonny Evans all played for the youth and then the first team.

MASTER MOURINHO

In his five full seasons at Chelsea, Jose Mourinho won the league title three times. He arrived at Old Trafford in 2016 after also picking up the title in Portugal, Spain and Italy. Mourinho has two Champions League victories as well – he really is one of the best bosses in the 21st century! He's already worked his magic at Manchester United, with the Europa League and EFL Cup, and is desperate to land the club's first title since 2013.

STAT ATTACK

Manchester United's Premier League statistics and numbers don't lie – their amazing numbers show why they are the most successful team of the last 25 years. Since 1992 they have won over 620 points, which is about 80 more than Arsenal and Chelsea behind them, with a record 430+ clean sheets. They have the biggest home win (9–0) and the biggest away win (8–1) in the League. Manchester United's stats are staggering!

ALL ABOUT ARSENAL

Arsenal have played in every Premier League season, fielded some of the game's greatest players, and have won over 30 honours.

TROPHY TALK

Arsenal won the Premier League three times between 1998 and 2004 and had a record 13 FA Cup final victories up to 2017. Their fans are disappointed that they haven't won the League for a long time, but The Gunners did come close to the Champions League crown after losing the Final to Barcelona in 2006. Coming fifth in 2017 was the first time they had finished outside the top four since 1996.

GAME PLAN

Arsenal are famous for playing attractive, attacking football under manager Arsene Wenger. Most of their play goes through Germany midfielder Mesut Ozil, who is a master of goal assists, with pacey goal-getters Pierre-Emerick Aubameyang or Alex Lacazette leading the line.

STARS TO WATCH...

PIERRE-EMERICK AUBAMEYANG
FORWARD
Quick & lethal shooting

MESUT OZIL
MIDFIELDER
Magical left foot

LAURENT KOSCIELNY
CENTRE-BACK
Cuts out danger

HENRIKH MKHITARYAN
MIDFIELDER
Incredible control & passing

NICKNAME: The Gunners
STADIUM: The Emirates Stadium
CAPACITY: 59,867
HOME KIT: Red shirt & white shorts
YEAR FOUNDED: 1886
CLUB LEGENDS: Thierry Henry, Ian Wright, Patrick Vieira, Tony Adams, Dennis Bergkamp, Liam Brady

PLAYER POWER

The Gunners have splashed out on star attacking players in recent years, including Aubameyang and Lacazette who together cost over £100 million. Henrikh Mkhitaryan joined in Janaury 2018 from Manchester United and is a goalscorer and creator to star alongside Ozil in midfield. Hector Bellerin is one of the quickest and most effective right-backs in the Premier League.

> Room for me too, please!

> **Arsene Wenger** took charge of Arsenal in October **1996**, before Gunners midfielder Ainsley Maitland-Niles was even born!

BIG BUY: Pierre-Emerick Aubameyang (**£56m** in 2018) **BARGAIN BUY:** Aaron Ramsey (**£5m** in 2008)
BIGGEST PREM WIN: 7–3 v Newcastle United (2012) **FAMOUS GAME:** 2–2 v Spurs to win the title in **2004**

ARSENAL

GREAT GUNNERS!

Arsenal fans are treated to some exciting footy at Emirates Stadium and have a team loaded with superstars, plus a manager with the most experience in the Premier League.

FAB FRENCHMAN

Arsenal have a wonderful history of super-skilled Frenchman scoring and creating goals for the team. Thierry Henry, Sylvain Wiltord, Nicolas Anelka and Robert Pires are all Gunners' legends. In February 2018, Laurent Koscielny made his own bit of history by scoring his 19th league goal. That made him the club's highest-scoring defender in the Premier League.

DOUBLE TROUBLE

Pierre-Emerick Aubameyang and Henrik Mkhitaryan played together at Borussia Dortmund for three seasons. They formed a lethal double act, with Mkhitaryan setting up loads of goals and chances for the speedy striker to tuck away. In their final season together they struck 59 goals and 31 assists. So it's no surprise to see them doing exactly the same at Arsenal now – in their first game together, Mkhitaryan set up Auba's goal!

> Arsenal have made the most team passes in Premier League history – over **238,800!**

CECH IT OUT

Arsenal have one of the finest Premier League goalkeepers of all time. Petr Cech won four titles with Chelsea before his switch across London in 2015, winning his fifth FA Cup with Arsenal in just his second season. He's also the only keeper to record more than 199 clean sheets in the Premier League. The big stopper also has four Golden Glove awards, which are given to the keeper with the most clean sheets at the end of the season.

WENGER'S EPIC RECORD

No other manager has taken charge of more Premier League games than Arsene Wenger. He set the record with his 811th game with Arsenal on 31 December 2017, with his first back on 12 October 1996. By February 2018 he had picked up 470 league wins, 13 Manager of the Month awards and three Manager of the Season trophies. He's tied with Manchester United's Jose Mourinho on three Premier League championships.

Fancy a half-time cup of tea and biscuit?

EXCITING EMIRATES

Arsenal moved into Emirates Stadium in 2006, but their best run of games at the ground didn't come until more than ten years later. They set a record run of Premier League wins at the stadium between April and November 2017, when they won 12 games in a row. That included victories over Manchester United, Spurs, Leicester City and Everton. Emirates Stadium has finally become a fortress for The Gunners!

18 EPIC FACTS!

Have you heard of the exciting Premier League Under-18s competition? Here we reveal the talented superkids and the teams involved in this epic event.

2 TWIN TROPHIES!

There are two awesome trophies up for grabs. The winner of the north and south group receive a shield, with a big trophy (which looks similar to the real Premier League trophy) given to the overall champs. Double delight!

1 TOP 12!

There are 12 teams in the Premier League Under-18s south group, including Chelsea, Tottenham Hotspur, Arsenal, Leicester City, Aston Villa and Southampton. Manchester United, Manchester City, Liverpool FC and Everton are part of the 12-team north group.

3 FIERCE FINAL!

The winners of the north and south group then meet for a deciding match to see who's crowned the overall Premier League Under-18s champion. Chelsea, Manchester City, Middlesbrough, Everton and Fulham have all taken the title in the past.

4 LIVERPOOL FC LEGEND!

The Liverpool FC Under-18s team manager is Steven Gerrard – one of the best Liverpool FC players ever! Gerrard took charge of the side in the summer of 2017 and the young Reds were undefeated in their first 12 League games under him.

5 AWESOME ANGEL!

Manchester United Under-18 playmaker, Angel Gomes, became the first player born in the 21st century to appear in the Premier League. In May 2017, aged 16 years and 263 days, he played for Jose Mourinho's Red Devils against Crystal Palace.

6 BRILLIANT BREWSTER!

Although he only turned 18 in April 2018 and was young enough to be part of last season's Under-18 team, Liverpool FC striker Rhian Brewster was actually in The Reds' first team last season. He also made his debut for the Under-23s aged just 16!

7 MARCUS MAKES HIS MARK!

Marcus Rashford began 2015–16 with Manchester United's Under-18s, but finished it as a first-team star at Old Trafford. Rashford burst into the Red Devil's Premier League squad, scoring eight goals between February and May. He won the FA Cup too!

9 KEEP COUNTING!

Defenders, midfielders and strikers must be part of the Under-18 age category to represent a club at this level. But goalkeepers from the Under-19 group can still play in the Premier League.

8 FOOTY LEAGUE LADS!

In the 2017–18 season there were nine clubs from the Championship and League 1 competing in the Under-18s event. These included Norwich City, Sunderland, Derby County, Blackburn Rovers, Middlesbrough and Reading.

10 GOALS GALORE!

Arsenal and Chelsea's Under-18s teams both smashed in the goals in 2017–18, scoring 46 after just 15 league games. Chelsea beat West Ham United 7–0, Fulham 6–1 and Swansea City 5–0 and 5–1!

12 BARLOW BAGS DEAL!

After making 19 appearances, scoring 12 goals and making three assists for the Under-18s, Manchester United's Aidan Barlow signed his first professional deal with the club at Christmas in 2017. Manager Jose Mourinho is a big fan of the attacking midfielder.

13 BLUES BROTHERS!

Chelsea's Under-18s midfielder George McEachran is the brother of Josh McEachran, who made 11 Premier League appearances for Chelsea. George has already won the Premier League Under-18s title and FA Youth Cup with The Blues.

11 LEAGUE 2!

The Premier League 2 is just like the Under-18s league, except the age limit is for Under-23 players. There is a Division 1 and Division 2. Everton were crowned Division 1 champions in 2017, with Swansea City lifting the Division 2 award.

14 VILLA THRILLERS!

Aston Villa enjoyed a good season in the Championship in 2017–18 and made a great push for promotion. Steve Bruce's team had several talented lads who had played for the Premier League Under-18s, with Easah Suliman, Mitch Clark, Jake Doyle-Hayes and Callum O'Hare all making their first-team debuts!

15 FIVE STAR!

An incredible five players who have starred for Everton's Under-18s made their first team debuts in the same game in December 2017! Harry Charsley, Fraser Hornby, Nathan Broadhead, Alex Denny and Anthony Gordon all played in The Toffees' 3–0 win over Apollon Limassol in the Europa League.

16 CUP KIDS!

Some Premier League Under-18s players will also star in an exciting new competition called the Premier League Cup, which began in 2016. It's mainly for Under-23 teams and 32 clubs compete in eight groups of four, with the top two from each reaching the knockout rounds. Swansea City were winners in 2017.

I'll show this off to all me mates!

17 EPIC BICYCLE KICK!

Southampton defender Kayne Ramsay netted one of the goals of the season in 2018 with a superb overhead bicycle kick against Tottenham Hotspur. Ramsay says his hero is Real Madrid captain Sergio Ramos. Well, Ramos would have loved to score like Ramsay did!

18 ACE AWARDS!

Just like in the Premier League, there's even a special Premier League 2 Player of the Season and Player of the Month award. Swansea City striker Oliver McBurnie was awarded the best player prize in 2017, beating stars like Liverpool FC's Trent Alexander-Arnold and Manchester United's Axel Tuanzebe.

GET TO THE GROUND!

Do you think you know your way around the Scottish Premiership? Head to the START, then follow the yellow lines to find a route to each super stadium!

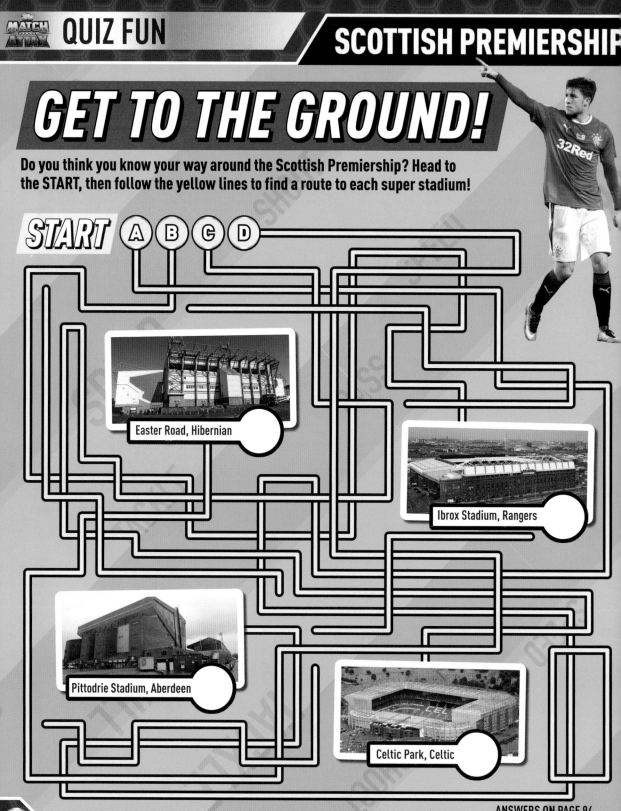

START Ⓐ Ⓑ Ⓒ Ⓓ

Easter Road, Hibernian

Ibrox Stadium, Rangers

Pittodrie Stadium, Aberdeen

Celtic Park, Celtic

ANSWERS ON PAGE 94.

KEVIN DE BRUYNE

If you want to be a proper Premier League footy fan, you also need to know about the top stars from years gone past. This bunch is the best!

BLASTS FROM THE PAST

DIDIER DROGBA
STRIKER
CLUB: Chelsea

Easily the most popular Chelsea striker of the last 20 years, Drogba struck 164 goals in just 381 games for The Blues. He bagged four Premier League crowns, four FA Cups, three League Cups and the Champions League in a trophy-packed career. The powerful goal machine also won two Premier League Golden Boots.

With goals, is Chelsea's top scorer in European footy.

MICHAEL OWEN
STRIKER
CLUBS: Liverpool FC, Newcastle United, Manchester United, Stoke City

At Anfield and Old Trafford, speedy striker Owen is worshipped for the goals he scored and trophies he won. He shot to stardom as a teenage terror and hit 118 Premier League goals for Liverpool FC before winning the title at Manchester United in 2011. With England, Owen recorded an impressive 40 goals in 89 games.

ASHLEY COLE
LEFT-BACK
CLUBS: Arsenal, Chelsea
Probably the Premier League's No.1 left-back, Cole played nearly 400 games for Chelsea and Arsenal in the league. Famous for his speed and energy in attack – and for defending like a brick wall, the England legend has 107 caps, three League titles and a record seven FA Cup victories.

Great goals, great hair – I've got the lot!

DAVID BECKHAM
WINGER
CLUB: Manchester United
These days he's a huge celebrity, TV star and underpants model, but don't forget that 'Becks' was a mega player for Manchester United between 1995 and 2003. His crossing, free-kicks and hard work were legendary and he helped The Red Devils to six championships, two FA Cups and the Champions League. His skills were definitely not 'pants'!

DENNIS BERGKAMP
FORWARD
CLUB: Arsenal
Bergkamp was one of Arsenal's great Premier League goalscorers, alongside legends like Ian Wright and Thierry Henry. The Dutchman's classy footwork and fantastic vision made him a nightmare for defenders. His 2002 goal against Newcastle United, where he spun the ball past a defender before a side foot finish, was stunning.

ALAN SHEARER
STRIKER
CLUBS: Blackburn Rovers, Newcastle United
Shearer's single championship medal may be outnumbered by the medals of Keane, Giggs and Vieira, but he had just as much impact on the Premier League. His game plan was all about goals – Big Al scored long-range stunners, headers, penalties, free-kicks and tap-ins. A sensation in front of goal.

Cole joined Manchester United in **1995** from Newcastle United for a then record **£7 million**.

I need a calculator to add up all my goals!

ANDY COLE

STRIKER

CLUBS: Newcastle United, Manchester United, Blackburn Rovers, Fulham, Manchester City, Portsmouth, Sunderland

In the late 1990s, Cole was one of the most feared strikers in the land. Blessed with pace and power, he won five titles between 1996 and 2001 with Manchester United. Cole's the third highest scorer in the Premier League with 187 goals from 414 appearances.

PATRICK VIEIRA

MIDFIELDER

CLUBS: Arsenal, Manchester City

With all-action midfielder Patrick Vieira leading the team, Arsenal were crowned Champions in 1998, 2002 and 2004. Vieira combined English-style power with French flair and skills. In 2001 he was named Premier League Player of the Season and was part of the unbeaten Invincibles team in 2003–2004.

CRISTIANO RONALDO

WINGER/STRIKER

CLUB: Manchester United

Manchester United fans think of Ronaldo as their best-ever Premier League player. Between 2003 and 2009, the Portuguese master amazed the crowds with 84 goals in 196 League games and three championship wins. Ronaldo became the most feared striker in the world and keepers had no chance when he unleashed his magic!

PAUL SCHOLES

MIDFIELDER

CLUB: Manchester United

Playing alongside greats like Ronaldo, Beckham, Rooney and Cantona, Scholes never stole the spotlight, but was just as vital to Manchester United's success between 1995 and 2013. In 499 League games the attacking midfielder scored 107 goals, racking up 11 League titles and also pocketing two Champions Leagues and three FA Cups.

LUIS SUAREZ

STRIKER

CLUB: Liverpool FC

Suarez smashing goal after goal in the red of Liverpool FC was a familiar sight between 2011 and 2014. In his last season at Anfield, before joining Barcelona for £65 million, he banged in 31 to land the Golden Boot as The Reds just failed to win their first Premier League title. Suarez's finishing and accuracy were out of this world.

Suarez's Premier League goal record is one of the best ever with **69** in just **110** games.

STEVEN GERRARD

MIDFIELDER

CLUB: Liverpool FC

Despite never winning the Premier League in 17 seasons, Stevie G is still worshipped as a legend in the competition. His all-round midfield skills meant he could score stunning match-winners, boss the pitch and captain The Reds with style and never-ending energy. His 120 goals in 504 League games is simply superb.

RYAN GIGGS

MIDFIELDER

CLUB: Manchester United

No Premier League player can match Giggs's medal count! As a flying left winger who developed into a silky-smooth central midfielder, the Welsh wizard won 13 League titles, four FA Cups, three League Cups and two Champions League. He even managed Manchester United, the only club he played for, for a few games in 2014.

Bale blasted an incredible **21** League goals in each of his last two seasons at Spurs.

TEDDY SHERINGHAM
STRIKER
CLUBS: Nottingham Forest, Tottenham Hotspur, Manchester United, Portsmouth, West Ham United
A clever striker with sharp moves and cool finishing in the box, Sheringham scored for five Premier League clubs. He had most success at Spurs and Manchester United, winning the Golden Boot and three League titles. He is the Premier League's oldest goalscorer at 40 years and 268 days.

JOHN TERRY
CENTRE-BACK
CLUB: Chelsea
With over 700 appearances, including more than 500 with the captain's armband, Terry is the most successful leader in Chelsea's history. A centre-back with terrific tackling, heading and passing skills, he scooped four Premier League medals, five FA Cups, the Champions League and Europa League.

That's another trophy in the bag!

GARETH BALE
WINGER
CLUB: Tottenham Hotspur
Before his world record £85-million move to Real Madrid in 2013, Bale was the Premier League's most eye-catching player. The Welsh winger was an unstoppable force for Spurs with dazzling skills and superhuman speed. His lethal left foot could do anything with the ball.

GIANFRANCO ZOLA
FORWARD
CLUB: Chelsea
You didn't have to be a Chelsea fan to appreciate the tricks, goals and epic attacking talent of this little Italian. Zola danced through defences and loved to beat keepers with a classy finish from inside – or outside – the box. He won five major cups with the Blues between 1997 and 2000.

FRANK LAMPARD

MIDFIELDER

CLUBS: West Ham United, Chelsea, Manchester City

Few players have ever had the midfield talent of Lampard. Between 2001 and 2014, he scored a record 211 goals in 648 games for Chelsea to win three championships, four FA Cups, two League Cups and the Champions League. Lamps was a goalscorer, a goal creator and playmaker all rolled into one.

I was a Highbury hero!

THIERRY HENRY

STRIKER

CLUB: Arsenal

Henry was a great goalscorer... and a scorer of great goals! He became a superstar at Arsenal after joining in 1999 and went on to win the title twice, two FA Cups and helped The Gunners reach their first Champions League Final. He also lifted the World Cup and Euros trophy with France in a career stuffed with silverware and achievements.

Henry's best season was in **2003-04**, with **30** Premier League goals.

ERIC CANTONA

FORWARD

CLUBS: Leeds United, Manchester United

Cantona only played for Manchester United between 1992 and 1997, but those five years were packed with incredible goals. The fantastic France forward was a four-time Premier League champion and amazed the Old Trafford crowd with top-class displays. Another legendary Manchester United No.7.

ROY KEANE

MIDFIELDER

CLUBS: Nottingham Forest, Manchester United

One of the toughest and most competitive players to appear in the Premier League, Keane's game was built around energy, power, tackling and passing. With Beckham, Scholes, Giggs and Butt alongside him, Keane captained one of the best midfields ever seen in the Premier League.

Here are four fun puzzles, all about the guys who grab goals every week in the Premier League.

GOAL GRABBERS!

MISSING LETTERS
Some letters have dropped off these shirts – what are the names of these players?

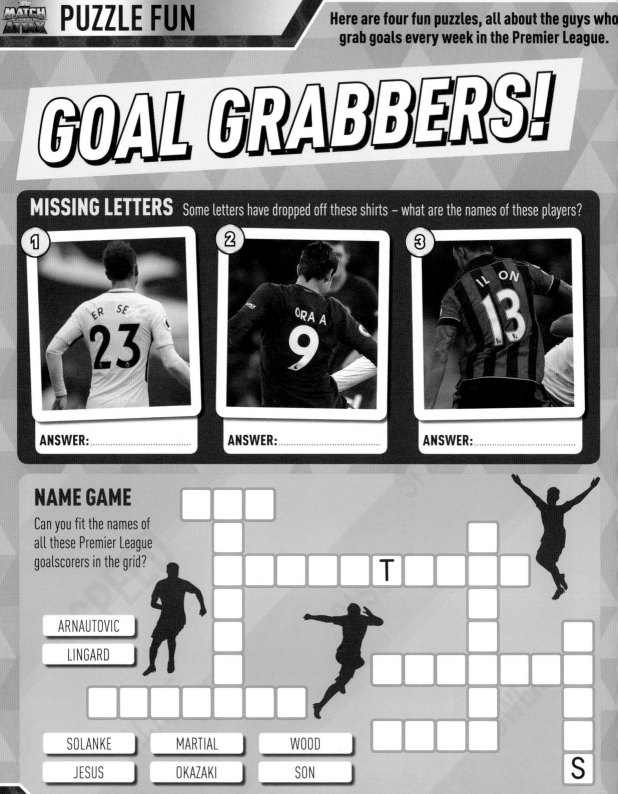

① ER SE 23

ANSWER:................................

② ORA A 9

ANSWER:................................

③ IL ON 13

ANSWER:................................

NAME GAME

Can you fit the names of all these Premier League goalscorers in the grid?

T

S

ARNAUTOVIC

LINGARD

SOLANKE

JESUS

MARTIAL

OKAZAKI

WOOD

SON

PAYING THE PENALTY

Arsenal striker Alex Lacazette scores a penalty against The Baggies, but which ball is the real deal?

THE REAL BALL IS:

GUESS THE YEAR

In which year were these goals scored? Pick from these options! → **2016 2017 2018**

Andy Carroll unleashes a fierce volley for West Ham United against Arsenal.

ANSWER:............................ .

Aguero opens the scoring for Manchester City against Burnley.

ANSWER:...

Firmino fires a shot past Arsenal in the Premier League.

ANSWER:...

ANSWERS ON PAGE 94.

BUILD THE ULTIMATE PLAYER

Now you can create the greatest player ever!

Pick the best player from each list, or choose your own to build a superstar with speed, power, goals and vision...

THE HEADING OF...

Peter CROUCH ☐
Virgil VAN DIJK ☐
Olivier GIROUD ☐
Christian BENTEKE ☐

Other: ....

THE SPEED OF...

Pierre-Emerick AUBAMEYANG ☐
Theo WALCOTT ☐
Leroy SANE ☐
Wilfried ZAHA ☐

Other:

THE STRENGTH OF...

Vincent KOMPANY ☐
Wayne ROONEY ☐
Victor WANYAMA ☐
Romelu LUKAKU ☐

Other:

THE RIGHT FOOT OF...

Eden HAZARD ☐
Harry KANE ☐
Jamie VARDY ☐
Sergio AGUERO ☐

Other:

THE LEFT FOOT OF...

Mesut OZIL ☐
Riyad MAHREZ ☐
Mohamed SALAH ☐
David SILVA ☐

Other: ....

PAUL POGBA

ALL ABOUT CELTIC

The green and white of Celtic is famous around the world. Discover facts and stats about this legendary Scottish club.

TROPHY TALK

Celtic continue to dominate the Scottish Premiership and cup competitions. The Glasgow giants won six titles in a row between 2012 and 2017, picking up five Scottish Cups and League Cups in that time too. Manager Brendan Rodgers has been very successful at Celtic Park since 2016 and took his team on a 69-game unbeaten run in Scottish games between 2016 and 2017.

GAME PLAN

Celtic's style is to play attacking football. Even in the Champions League, where they've had tough games against huge teams like PSG, Bayern Munich and Barcelona in recent years, The Bhoys always get forward and try to score, rather than defend with ten players. Skilful wingers and forwards, like James Forrest and Scott Sinclair, are exciting on the ball and pop up with goals all the time.

STARS TO WATCH...

JAMES FORREST
WINGER
Goalscoring right-footer

SCOTT SINCLAIR
FORWARD
Eye-catching skills & goals

CRAIG GORDON
GOALKEEPER
Powerful & experienced

OLIVIER NTCHAM
MIDFIELDER
Hardworking goal creator

NICKNAME: The Bhoys
STADIUM: Celtic Park
CAPACITY: 60,411
HOME KIT: Green & white hooped shirt, white shorts
YEAR FOUNDED: 1887
CLUB LEGENDS: Henrik Larsson, Jimmy Johnstone, Jimmy McGrory, Bobby Murdoch, Kenny Dalglish

PLAYER POWER

In 2017–18 Celtic shared the goals around their team, with Forrest, Sinclair and striker Leigh Griffiths both well into double figures. Young left-back Kieran Tierney has shot to stardom since Rodgers took over and French forward Moussa Dembele is another net-buster. Celtic work hard as a team and their never-give-up attitude has won them points aplenty!

Magic Moussa strikes again!

Scott Brown played his **400th** game for Celtic in January 2018.

BIG BUY: Olivier Ntcham (**£4.5m** in 2017) **BARGAIN BUY:** Dedryck Boyata (**£1.5m** in 2015) **CAPTAIN:** Scott Brown
BIGGEST LEAGUE WIN (since 1998): **9-0** v Aberdeen (2010) **FAMOUS WIN:** v Barcelona in **2012**

GLASGOW GIANTS!

CELTIC v PREMIER LEAGUE

Celtic fans often wonder how their team would get on in England's Premier League. Well, their record against English teams in European football is pretty good. They've beaten Manchester United, Liverpool FC, Blackburn Rovers and Leeds United in the past. In the 2016–17 season, Celtic secured two thrilling draws against Manchester City.

BRILLIANT BROWN

Captain Scott Brown joined Celtic in 2007 for £4.4 million from Hibernian, which was a record transfer between Scottish clubs. He became captain in 2010 and has over 15 major trophies with the club. In December 2017 he set another record by playing in his 69th Champions League game for Celtic – no other Scottish player has made more appearances in Europe's top competition.

TEN TARGET

Celtic and Rangers have both won Scotland's top league nine times in a row, with Celtic achieving it between 1966 and 1974. Winning the Premiership in 2018 was The Bhoys' seventh in a row, but their ultimate target is to finally land ten consecutive titles. However, Rangers, Aberdeen, Hibs and Hearts will be out to stop them!

BECOMING SAINTS

Southampton have splashed out on some of Celtic's biggest stars. Virgil van Djik left Celtic for The Saints for £11.5 million before joining Liverpool FC in 2018 for £75 million – a world record for a defender. Goalkeeper Fraser Forster and midfielder Victor Wanyama also moved to St. Mary's for a total of £22.5 million and are now Premier League heroes. Celtic made millions from the smart transfer moves!

QUALITY KIDS

Celtic Park is home to many top-quality young players with a massive future. Kieran Tierney has already captained Celtic and Scotland and became a big part of the treble-winning team in 2017. Norwegian defender or midfielder Kris Ajer turned 20 in 2018 and Kouassi Eboue is set to become a key midfielder after his £3 million arrival from FK Krasnodar.

Celtic manager **Brendan Rodgers** also took Swansea into the Premier League in 2011, becoming the first Welsh club to achieve it.

ALL ABOUT RANGERS

In the blue half of Glasgow, Rangers have a record number of league titles and a fantastic history. Here, you can take a closer look at the mighty Gers!

GAME PLAN

Rangers have a strong mix of experience and exciting young talent in their squad. Manager Graeme Murty took charge of the team in October 2017 and often played a bold diamond formation in midfield, with young defender or midfielder Ross McCrorie at the base. Right-back James Tavernier loves to attack and score goals, linking up with Daniel Candeias on the wing.

TROPHY TALK

Rangers proudly boast the most Scottish top league titles, picking up their 54th victory in 2011. They first won the league in 1891. The Gers also have 33 Scottish Cup wins between 1894 and 2009, 27 League Cup wins and the European Cup Winners' Cup from 1972. Rangers have won the most league titles of any professional club in the world – including Barcelona, Real Madrid, Juventus and Bayern Munich!

STARS TO WATCH...

JAMES TAVERNIER
RIGHT-BACK
Quick & ready to attack

ALFREDO MORELOS
STRIKER
Smart around the box

ROSS McCRORIE
DEFENDER/MIDFIELDER
Powerful & composed

GRAHAM DORRANS
MIDFIELDER
Creative goalscorer

NICKNAME: The Gers
STADIUM: Ibrox
CAPACITY: 50,817
HOME KIT: Royal blue shirts & white shorts
YEAR FOUNDED: 1873
CLUB LEGENDS: Jim Baxter, Ally McCoist, Richard Gough, Brian Laudrup, Davie Cooper, John Greig

PLAYER POWER

Colombian striker Alfredo Morelos is making a big name for himself at Ibrox after joining in summer 2017. He scored eight in his first nine games and was a great strike partner for Kenny Miller. Graham Dorrans has had injury problems, but is a big attacking threat from midfield. Defender Lee Wallace has captained The Gers bravely, with Jason Holt and Portugal centre-back Bruno Alves also wearing the armband in 2017 and 2018.

I win the scary face competition!

The attendance of   at Ibrox in   , against Celtic, is a British league record.

BIG BUY: Eduardo Herrera (**£1.5m** in 2017) **BARGAIN BUY:** James Tavernier (**£200,000** in 2015) **CAPTAIN:** Lee Wallace
BIGGEST PREM WIN (since 1998): **7–0** v St Johnstone (1998) **FAMOUS WIN:** v Celtic to win the title in 1999

READY FOR SUCCESS

Here are five things to know about Rangers, including a fierce rivalry with Celtic, their battle back to the Premiership and the top-quality players in their first team.

BACK AT THE TOP

After financial problems, Rangers made their way back into the Scottish Premiership in 2016 following four years outside the top division. They're desperate to add to their record score of titles and for success in cup finals as the club restores itself to glory. Stopping Celtic from sweeping up the silverware is their main target!

ACE ACADEMY

With Rangers not able to spend huge transfer fees compared to Premier League and other European teams, developing great academy players has become vital to the club. Their Murray Park academy opened in 2001 and by 2018 had produced around 50 first team players. Forward Ryan Hardie played for the first-team in 2017–18 after coming through the academy and Ross McCrorie, another academy star, has been tipped to become a future Rangers captain.

KING KENNY

Scotland striker Kenny Miller amazingly joined Rangers three times, and is also one of just five players since 1945 to have played for The Gers and Celtic. He first moved to Ibrox in 2000 and also played between 2008 and 2011, when he won three titles in a row and two cups. The experienced star joined the club again in 2014 and scored his 100th goal for Rangers in 2016.

SUPER SKIPPER

Lee Wallace has been with Rangers since 2011, joining for £1.5 million from Hearts, and stayed with the club as it battled back from the Third Division to the Premiership. In his first season the left-back wowed the Rangers fans with a stunning strike in a 3–2 win over Celtic and made his 250th appearance for The Gers in 2017. Wallace's spirit and passion are key to Rangers' hopes of collecting more trophies.

I can't run unless I stick my thumbs up. Weird!

With **355** goals, **Rangers'** all-time top scorer is Ally McCoist. He also managed Rangers between 2011 and 2014.

CITY RIVALS

The Celtic v Rangers games are some of the fiercest and most exciting derby games in the world – every bit as thrilling as Arsenal v Spurs, Liverpool FC v Everton and Inter v AC Milan! The games are known as 'Old Firm' matches and Ibrox is packed out when Celtic visit. In 2011 a 0–0 draw with Celtic helped Rangers win the last of their 54 titles in what was also legendary manager Walter Smith's final Old Firm game.

Goals, games, wins, assists... these Premier League heroes have smashed lots of records! Check out the facts and stats that make them record-breakers.

RECORD BREAKERS

CARDS AND GAMES

Ex-England midfielder Gareth Barry holds two Premier League records – including one that he doesn't want! Playing for Aston Villa, Manchester City, Everton and West Bromwich Albion, Barry has played over 650 games, which is more than anyone else, but has also been shown over 120 yellow cards. Referees have no probs spelling his name!

HAT-TRICK HERO MANE

Speedy Liverpool FC forward Sadio Mane zoomed into the record books with a quick-fire hat-trick in 2015. Playing for Southampton against Aston Villa, Mane took just two minutes and 56 seconds between scoring his first and third goals, shaving more than 90 seconds off the previous record set in 1994.

CITY'S SUPER STREAK

High-flying Manchester City were the team to catch in 2017–18 and seemed to have the title won by the time they tucked into Christmas dinner! Their all-conquering streak saw them win 18 league games in a row between August and December, which set a sensational Premier League record. The perfect Christmas prezzie for their fans!

SAM'S SUPER SEVEN

Sam has had more clubs than a golfer! He's managed Bolton Wanderers, Newcastle United, Blackburn Rovers, West Ham United, Sunderland, Crystal Palace and Everton in the Premier League. His first game came back in 2001.

DEADLY DOUBLE CENTURY

Wayne Rooney is one of only a couple of current Premier League player to have scored more than 200 League goals. The Everton goal machine struck 183 times for Manchester United and over 25 times for The Toffees. Alan Shearer has the overall record with 260 for Newcastle United and Blackburn Rovers between 1992 and 2006.

Woo hoo! I'm a scarecrow!

Rooney scored his 200th league goal for Everton against Manchester City in 2017.

UNBEATEN ARSENAL

Arsene Wenger's Arsenal are the only Premier League side to go all season without losing in the League. Between August 2003 and May 2004, The Gunners had zero defeats, winning 26 and drawing 12 as they picked up the title with ease.

MORE PREMIER LEAGUE RECORDS...

FEWEST WINS IN A SEASON: Derby County (1 win in 2007–08)
HIGHEST ATTENDANCE: 81,978 (Tottenham Hotspur v Manchester United, 2018)
MOST GOAL ASSISTS: Ryan Giggs (162 for Manchester United)
PLAYED IN EVERY PREMIER LEAGUE SEASON: Manchester United, Arsenal, Chelsea, Liverpool FC, Tottenham Hotspur, Everton

I'm head and shoulders above the rest!

HEADING FOR GOAL

Giant striker Peter Crouch holds a BIG Premier League record. The Stoke City star had notched up over 50 headed goals by 2018, which is more than Alan Shearer, Dion Dublin and Les Ferdinand. Crouch also holds the record for most substitute appearances, with 147 by February 2018.

AGUERO'S FAB FOUR

In 2018, Manchester City's Sergio Aguero scored four goals in a 5–1 win against Leicester City. He became the first player to score four or more goals three times in a single Premier League game. In 2015 he grabbed FIVE goals against Newcastle United!

FOXES' FAVE

Leicester's Jamie Vardy has scored in a record 11 Premier League games in a row. The striker scored 13 in those games, between August and November 2015. In 2018 he also became the first player to score against Arsenal, Chelsea, Liverpool FC, Tottenham Hotspur, Manchester City and Manchester United in the same season.

MAGIC LAMPS

Who do you think has scored the most Premier League goals from outside the penalty box? Shearer, Henry or Kane perhaps? Nope. It's former West Ham United, Chelsea and Manchester City goalscoring midfielder Frank Lampard. Lethal Lamps struck a record 41 times from distance.

I'm all about the goals. Goals. goals. goals. goals. goals!

WIN KINGS

Manchester United are the only team with more than 600 Premier League wins in total. By February 2018 they had won over 620 games, with second-placed Arsenal having 83 less wins than The Red Devils. Chelsea were third with 531 victories, followed by Liverpool FC (492) and Tottenham Hotspur (415).

DUNNE IT AGAIN

Former Premier League centre-back Richard Dunne hit a Premier League high of ten own goals between the 2004–05 and 2014–15 seasons. Dunne did the damage while at Manchester City, Aston Villa and QPR and he also has a joint record eight red cards in the League.

MORE PREMIER LEAGUE RECORDS...

MOST DEFEATS IN A ROW:	Sunderland (15 in 2002–03)
MOST GOALS CONCEDED IN A SEASON:	Swindon Town (100 in 1993–94)
MOST CLEAN SHEETS IN A SEASON:	Chelsea (25 in 2004–05)
MOST GAMES IN A ROW:	Brad Friedel (310 August 2004–October 2012)

EDEN HAZARD

ALL ABOUT
LIVERPOOL FC

With talented players, a fantastic stadium, special history and piles of trophies, Liverpool FC fans have lots of reasons to love their club!

TROPHY TALK

With over 40 major honours, Liverpool FC are one of the world's most successful clubs. The Anfield trophy cabinet includes 18 league titles, seven FA Cup wins between 1965 and 2006 and a record eight League Cups from 12 finals. In Europe, The Reds are Britain's best team thanks to five European Cups and Champions Leagues, three UEFA Cups and three UEFA Super Cups.

GAME PLAN

Manager Jurgen Klopp loves The Reds to burst forward – after Manchester City, Liverpool FC are probably the most attack-minded team in the Premier League. Their game plan sees a front three power towards the box, with quick and clever wide players supporting a central striker. A solid midfield protects the defence, which is marshalled by £75 million star Virgil van Dijk.

STARS TO WATCH...

MOHAMED SALAH
FORWARD
Can't stop scoring!

EMRE CAN
MIDFIELDER
Strong in defence & attack

ROBERTO FIRMINO
FORWARD
Skilful goalscorer

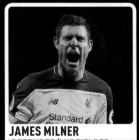

JAMES MILNER
DEFENDER/MIDFIELDER
Experienced & cool-headed

NICKNAME: The Reds
STADIUM: Anfield
CAPACITY: 53,314
HOME KIT: Red shirt & shorts
YEAR FOUNDED: 1892
CLUB LEGENDS: Steven Gerrard, Kenny Dalglish, Bill Shankly, Bob Paisley, Ian Rush, Roger Hunt

PLAYER POWER

The free-scoring forwards grab all the headlines for Liverpool FC! Mo Salah, Roberto Firmino and Sadio Mane link up like a dream in attack. The tricky trio blasted 56 goals in the first 37 games in 2017–18. Midfielders like Alex Oxlade-Chamberlain, Emre Can and Adam Lallana provide skill and power and young full-back Trent Alexander-Arnold has impressed with his energetic performances.

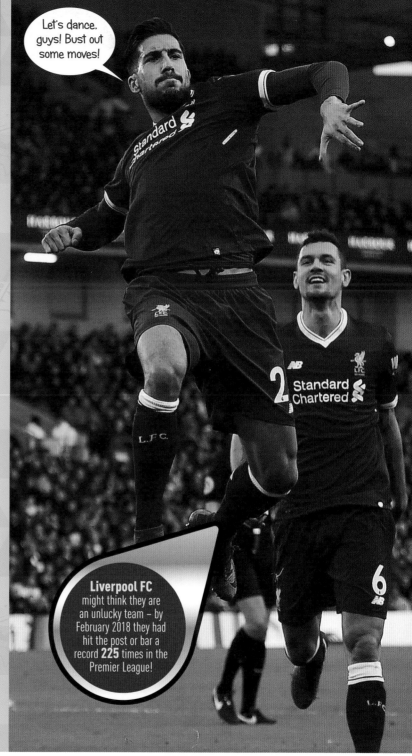

Let's dance, guys! Bust out some moves!

Liverpool FC might think they are an unlucky team – by February 2018 they had hit the post or bar a record **225** times in the Premier League!

BIG BUY: Virgil van Dijk (**£75m** in 2018) **BARGAIN BUY:** Joe Gomez (**£3.5m** 2015) **CAPTAIN:** Jordan Henderson
BIGGEST PREM WIN: 7–1 v Southampton (1999) **FAMOUS WIN:** v AC Milan in **2005** Champions League Final

LIVERPOOL FC

RED-Y TO ROCK

Liverpool FC have epic players and a truly special manager. Check out why The Reds are so great, and why trophies could soon be heading to Anfield.

KLOPP'S QUALITY

Before joining Liverpool FC in 2015, Jurgen Klopp had won the German Bundesliga twice and taken Borussia Dortmund to a Champions League Final. In his first season The Reds were runners-up in the League Cup and Europa League and he led Liverpool FC back into the Champions League in 2017. Klopp wants to finally make The Reds champions of England – it was 1990 when they last won the title.

HIDDEN GEMS

As well as buying superstars like Salah and Naby Kcita, Liverpool FC bag loads of transfer bargains. Joe Gomez, who can play centre-back and right-back, joined as a teenager from Charlton Athletic for just £3.5 million. Striker Dominic Solanke was snapped up from Chelsea and left-back Andrew Robertson was an £8 million steal from Hull City.

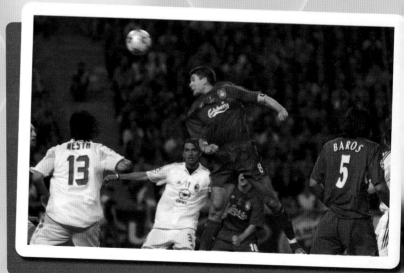

MAGIC MO-MENTS

There's no doubt who was Liverpool FC's star of 2017–18. Mo Salah was snapped up for £34 million last season and became an instant Anfield hero with electric displays in attack. The Egyptian's left foot is as good as Lionel Messi's and his playing style is just like the Barcelona ace, using speed, quick feet and laser shooting in front of goal. Salah's already worth more than double what The Reds paid for him!

FANTASTIC FANS

Liverpool FC players and visiting teams often say there's a special atmosphere created by the fans at Anfield. The ground is one of the best in the Premier League, with a great history, but with modern developments boosting the capacity to over 54,000. Before every game, The Reds' fans sing a famous song called 'You'll Never Walk Alone', which seems to fire up Salah, Firmino and the boys, ready for kick-off!

EPIC EURO STARS

Liverpool FC's European games are magical occasions, especially at Anfield. The club has an amazing record of winning European trophies, with 11 major honours since 1973. They won the greatest Champions League Final ever in 2005, beating AC Milan on penalties, and were runners-up again in 2007. Under the floodlights at Anfield, European games are usually spectacular and memorable.

Salah scored **21** goals in his first **25** Premier League games for Liverpool FC, which is even better than Reds' legends Robbie Fowler and Fernando Torres.

ALL ABOUT
TOTTENHAM HOTSPUR

Tottenham Hotspur are thrilling to watch, powered by goal machine Harry Kane at their brilliant new stadium. Let's dig deeper into the North London club!

GAME PLAN

With some of the best attacking midfielders in the Premier League, Tottenham Hotspur like to play with a defensive anchor – usually Eric Dier – and have a supporting trio behind lone striker Harry Kane. Spurs see action down the wings from full-backs Kieran Trippier and Danny Rose and are led at the back by the Belgian defensive duo of Toby Alderweireld and Jan Vertonghen.

TROPHY TALK

Tottenham Hotspur are one of 24 clubs to have won England's top division, taking the championship in 1961 and 1951. They became the first team to do the Double, which means winning the league and FA Cup in the same season. In total Spurs have eight FA Cup victories between 1901 and 1991, plus four League Cups. They were the first British team to secure a European trophy after success in the Cup Winners' Cup in 1963.

STARS TO WATCH...

HARRY WINKS
MIDFIELDER
Becoming a fans' fave

DELE ALLI
MIDFIELDER
Dribbles into the box

HUGO LLORIS
GOALKEEPER
Amazing acrobatic saves

HARRY KANE
STRIKER
Record-breaking goal-getter

NICKNAME: Spurs
STADIUM: The New White Hart Lane
CAPACITY: 62,062
HOME KIT: White shirt & navy shorts
YEAR FOUNDED: 1882
CLUB LEGENDS: Bill Nicholson, Jimmy Greaves, Glenn Hoddle, Ossie Ardiles, Ledley King

PLAYER POWER

As Kane causes havoc in attack, Dele Alli and Christian Eriksen unleash a lethal mix of dribbling, shooting and free-kick skills. Victor Wanyama's a midfield powerhouse and Belgium's Mousa Dembele is another attack-minded midfield star. Brazil winger Lucas Moura joined in 2018 for £25 million and adds pace and clever passing to Tottenham Hotspur's forward line.

> Kane? Nah. I'm Shouty McShout Face!

Tottenham Hotspur's Ledley King scored the fastest Premier League goal in 2000, after just ten seconds. **Christian Eriksen** scored after **10.5** seconds in 2018.

BIG BUY: Davinson Sanchez (**£42m** in 2017) **BARGAIN BUY:** Eric Dier (**£4m** in 2014) **CAPTAIN:** Hugo Lloris
BIGGEST PREM WIN: 9–1 v Wigan (2009) **FAMOUS WIN:** 5–1 v Arsenal in **2008** League Cup semi-final

SPURS SHOOTING HIGH!

Discover some top Spurs trivia, including Harry Kane's record year, Champions League glory and tense London rivalries.

GETTING GROUNDED

Tottenham Hotspur moved into their new 62,062 capacity stadium for the 2018–19 season after playing at Wembley while the old White Hart Lane ground was expanded and redeveloped. Spurs' new stadium is the biggest club ground in London and second only to Manchester United's near 75,000 capacity. It's a high-tech, high-quality complex that's perfect for the London hotshots – happy new home!

Dele signed for **Spurs** in 2015 for a modest £5 million, but has probably boosted his value twenty-fold thanks to a truly epic goalscoring ability.

Alli wears 'DELE' on his shirt.

REAL QUALITY

In recent seasons Tottenham Hotspur have been back in the Champions League. Their biggest win in 2017 was against reigning European and Spanish champions Real Madrid, whacking them 3–1 at Wembley. Spurs also did the double over German giants Borussia Dortmund that season to prove that they deserve to be mixing it with Europe's elite teams!

Whack! 'Ave some of this!

HUNDRED HERO KANE

In the 2017–18 season, superstar striker Harry Kane became Spurs' all-time top scorer in the Premier League and smashed the 100 league goal mark. The England hero netted a record 38 Premier League goals last year and was Europe's top scorer in 2017 with 56 goals in just 52 games for club and country. That was better than Lionel Messi, Cristiano Ronaldo and Robert Lewandowski!

SILVERWARE CHALLENGE

With an ace new stadium and a squad packed with quality players, Spurs know they should be challenging for – and winning – more trophies. Manager Mauricio Pochettino has turned Spurs into a top Premier League team – taking the title for the first time, and having success in the FA and League Cups, is definitely the target.

CAPITAL CLASHES

Tottenham Hotspur's rivalry with their North London neighbours Arsenal is one of the biggest in England. By the end of 2017, Spurs had won 11 Premier League games against Arsenal, with The Gunners ahead on 20 victories. Tottenham Hotspur haven't won both League games in the same season against their fiercest rivals since back in 1992–93. In the final North London derby at White Hart Lane last season, Spurs cruised to a 2–0 win with goals from Alli and Kane.

SHIRT SWAP

These 2018 Premier League stars have all swapped their shirts. Which players need to go with which kits?

①

ANSWER ....

②

ANSWER ....

③

ANSWER ....

④

ANSWER ....

⑤

ANSWER ....

⑥

ANSWER ....

MARKO ARNAUTOVIC

LUKA MILIVOJEVIC

NATHAN AKE

GERARD DEULOFEU

STEVEN DEFOUR

SHINJI OKAZAKI

ANSWERS ON PAGE 94.

SCOTT SINCLAIR

The FA Youth Cup is a fantastic trophy that every teenage player wants to get their hands on.

THE KIDS ARE UP FOR THE CUP!

Can't wait to bring the cup back to Manchester again!

Each season over 400 teams from England and Wales compete in knockout games in the FA Youth Cup. Under-18s teams can take part and the tournament first kicked off in 1952. The preliminary and qualifying rounds take place in September, with the two-legged final usually in May.

Chelsea have won the FA Youth Cup eight times between 1960 and 2017, dominating it since 2010. The young Blues won it that year and in 2012, 2014, 2015, 2016 and 2017. They were also runners-up to Norwich in 2013. Chelsea's biggest win over the two-legged final was 6–2 against Manchester City in 2017.

FINAL FACTS

West Ham United hold the record for the biggest winning scoreline in an FA Youth Cup final. Over two legs, The Hammers hammered Coventry City 9–0 in 1999! Future Premier League winners, and England internationals, Joe Cole and Michael Carrick were part of The Hammers' top teenage team.

Manchester United have the most final victories and picked up the cup ten times from 1953 to 2011. The Red Devils won the first five finals and even beat Cheshire team Nantwich 23–0 in one game during the 1952–53 season!

Chelsea won the 2015, 2016 and 2017 trophies by beating Manchester City every time in the final.

These Premier League stars have all lifted the FA Youth Cup in recent years with Chelsea...
- Ruben Loftus-Cheek
- Nathaniel Chalobah
- Nathan Ake
- Andreas Christensen
- Dominic Solanke
- Tammy Abraham

Other top players who have won the cup include...
- David Beckham
- Gary Neville
- Michael Owen
- Jamie Carragher
- George Best
- Paul Gascoigne
- David James
- Ryan Giggs

Help. I'm really flagging here!

Manchester United's awesome midfielders **Paul Pogba** and **Jesse Lingard** took the FA Youth Cup in 2011, after beating Sheffield United 6–3!

In FA Youth Cup finals, 13 is the record number of goals scored. In 2014, Chelsea won against Fulham 7–6 and in 1982 Watford beat Manchester United 7–6. Wolves saw off Chelsea 7–6 in 1958.

ALL ABOUT EVERTON

Take a tour around Everton and get to meet the club's big stars, plus plenty of fun facts, stats and numbers all about The Toffees.

TROPHY TALK

Everton fans unfortunately haven't seen much trophy success lately, with the 1995 FA Cup being their last major honour. But in the 1980s The Toffees took the league title twice, in 1985 and 1987, and the FA Cup in 1984 under legendary manager Howard Kendall. Everton have five FA Cup wins in total, plus the unwanted record of eight final losses, although they did win the European Cup Winners' Cup in 1985.

GAME PLAN

Everton have spent big money on exciting and skilful wingers and midfielders recently. When manager Sam Allardyce took control in 2017 he wanted to add pace to his team's attack, getting Yannick Bolasie flying down the touchline after injury and bringing Theo Walcott into the side. Everton have classy midfielders who can ping and pass the ball with ease to release strikers and wide players.

STARS TO WATCH...

GYLFI SIGURDSSON
MIDFIELDER
Passing & set-piece master

JORDAN PICKFORD
GOALKEEPER
Top England star

MICHAEL KEANE
CENTRE-BACK
Powerful tackling & heading

IDRISSA GUEYE
MIDFIELDER
Protects the defence

NICKNAME: The Toffees
STADIUM: Goodison Park
CAPACITY: 39,595
HOME KIT: Blue and white
YEAR FOUNDED: 1878
CLUB LEGENDS: Dixie Dean, Bob Latchford, Howard Kendall, Colin Harvey, Alan Ball

In **1933**, **Everton** were the first club to wear numbered shirts from one to **11** in a game.

PLAYER POWER

Allardyce is a manager who builds from his team's defence and wants to make sure that Everton keep a clean sheet before, hopefully, slotting in some goals! England goalkeeper Jordan Pickford is a superb stopper, with a strong backline in front of him that includes Ashley Williams, Michael Keane, Leighton Baines and club captain Phil Jagielka. Everton spent £27 million on Turkey striker Cenk Tosun in January 2018.

BIG BUY: Gylfi Sigurdsson (**£45m** in 2017) **BARGAIN BUY:** Seamus Coleman (**£60,000** in 2009) **BIGGEST PREM WINS:** **7-1** v Southampton (1996), **7-1** v Sunderland (2007) **FAMOUS WIN:** v Manchester United in **1995** FA Cup final

Everton have played in every Premier League season and have a famous history. Discover why the good times could soon be coming back!

TOFFEES LOOKING SWEET!

BIG SAM'S CHALLENGE

Sam Allardyce has been a manager for over 25 years, but in that time he's only won lower league titles and two Championship play-off trophies. Big Sam is desperate to finally win a major trophy and pick up Everton's first silverware since 1995. The club's owners, fans, players and the manager all want to see a cup added to the Goodison Park trophy cabinet!

GREAT GYLFI

Everton smashed their transfer record to bring Swansea's Gylfi Sigurdsson to Goodison Park for £45 million. The Iceland star is worth every penny because he's a midfield master with incredible passing and shooting skills who links defence and attack. In Sigurdsson's first 205 Premier League games he scored 45 goals, including 13 free-kicks and penalties, and made 36 assists.

Theo Walcott adds pace to the Blues' line-up.

WICKED WALCOTT

When England forward Theo Walcott joined Everton for £20 million in 2018 after 12 years at Arsenal, the fans were very excited! Walcott's one of the quickest players in the Premier League and can play anywhere across the attack. He's made over 270 league appearances, scored more than 65 goals and struck 18 times in the Champions League. He hit a match-winning double in just his second game for Everton. Get in!

TOP TOFFEES TALENT

With young heroes like Dominic Calvert-Lewin, Tom Davies, Jonjoe Kenny and Nikola Vlasic, Everton have a group of quality kids who could be stars for years to come. Energetic midfielder Davies joined the club as an 11 year-old and Calvert-Lewin's a strong attacker who scored for England in the 2017 Under-20 World Cup Final. Right-back Kenny captained Everton's Under-23 team to the Premier League 2 title in 2017.

ROONEY RETURNS

Wayne Rooney became a Premier League hero with Everton when he was only 16. The striker enjoyed two seasons at Goodison before playing for Manchester United for 13 years, but the boyhood Toffees fan returned in 2017. Rooney brings goals, vision and bags of experience and he absolutely loves wearing the blue shirt. Even when he was at Manchester United, he says he wore Everton pyjamas to bed!

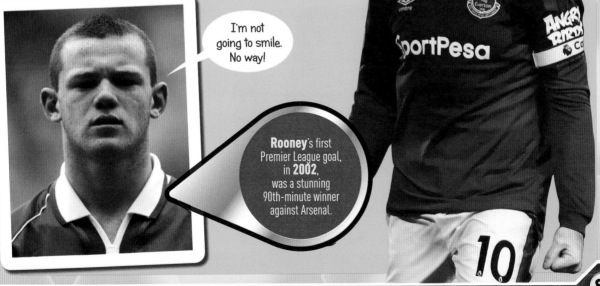

I'm not going to smile. No way!

Rooney's first Premier League goal, in **2002**, was a stunning 90th-minute winner against Arsenal.

CHANGING ROOM CHANGES

This is the Liverpool FC changing room before a big Premier League game. Can you spot all 10 differences made to the bottom picture?

1 2 3 4 5 6 7 8 9 10

CLUB GUIDE

ALL ABOUT

LEICESTER CITY

Leicester City are one of just six clubs to have won the Premier League and have built a brilliant team at the King Power Stadium. Don't miss these fab Foxes footy facts.

GAME PLAN

Under manager Claude Puel, Leicester City still rely on a speedy counter-attacking style that worked so well during the 2015–16 title-winning season. Away from home, The Foxes often sit a little deeper and use the tackling skills of midfielder Wilfred Ndidi in front of the back four. Leicester City's wingers are a key part of their game style, in support of a single or double strike force.

TROPHY TALK

There's only one place to start – Leicester City's mind-boggling Premier League championship victory in 2016! The Foxes, with Claudio Ranieri in charge, stormed to the title that season in one of the biggest shocks in world footy. The Foxes were worthy champions, though, finishing ten points ahead of second-placed Arsenal and beating Manchester City, Liverpool FC and Tottenham Hotspur along the way.

STARS TO WATCH...

JAMIE VARDY
STRIKER
Deadly in front of goal

ADRIEN SILVA
MIDFIELDER
All-round midfield skills

DEMARAI GRAY
WINGER
Speedy with top tricks

BEN CHILWELL
LEFT-BACK
Exciting & energetic

NICKNAME: The Foxes
STADIUM: King Power Stadium
CAPACITY: 32,273
HOME KIT: Blue shirt & shorts
YEAR FOUNDED: 1884
CLUB LEGENDS: Claudio Ranieri, Gary Lineker, Peter Shilton, Sep Smith, Muzzy Izzet

PLAYER POWER

Leicester City's rise to the top was built on true team spirit and a winning attitude, mixed with some incredible individual flair. Striker Jamie Vardy has been the club's goal hero since joining in 2012 and the attacking and set piece skills of Riyad Mahrez were key to their Premier League and Champions League successes. When stars like N'Golo Kante and Danny Drinkwater left, quality replacements like Wilfred Ndidi and Harry Maguire came in.

Leicester City lost just once in their first **16** league games when they won the title in 2016.

BIG BUY: Islam Slimani (**£29m** in 2016) **BARGAIN BUY:** Jamie Vardy (**£1m** in 2012) **CAPTAIN:** Wes Morgan
BIGGEST PREM WIN: 5–1 v QPR (2015) **FAMOUS WIN:** v Sevilla in **2017** to reach Champions League quarter-finals

These are exciting times for Leicester City fans. Check out some of the secrets behind the Foxes' success!

FOXES FLYING HIGH!

It's me. King Claudio!

Jamie Vardy is a speedy player – he's smashed **35 kilometres per hour** in Premier League games!

RANIERI REIGNS

The manager who masterminded Leicester City's rise to the Premier League crown was Claudio Ranieri. The likeable Italian, who has also managed Atletico Madrid, Chelsea, Juventus, Roma, Inter Milan and Nantes stormed to the title in his first season at the King Power Stadium and was named Manager of the Year. Sadly, he left the club in February 2017.

THANK YOU VARDY MUCH

You can see Jamie Vardy's Premier League stats and achievements on page 25, but Leicester City fans won't mind reading even more about their No.1 striker! Vardy's skill at racing behind defenders, stretching the opposition and shooting from inside and outside the box are legendary at the King Power Stadium. In December 2017 he netted his 50th Premier League goal in just 124 games.

FUTURE FOXES STARS

Drinkwater, Kante and other title-winning heroes may have left the King Power Stadium, but the club's brilliant youngsters means there's still plenty to smile about! Demarai Gray can play as a left winger or behind the striker and has been superb since signing from Birmingham City for a bargain £3.5 million in 2016. Ben Chilwell has a big future at left-back and exciting things are expected of £25-million striker Kelechi Iheanacho.

DOUBLE DELIGHT

For some of Leicester City's squad, winning the Premier League was their second medal with the club. The Foxes won the Championship in 2014 to take them back to the top division. Players like Vardy, Kasper Schmeichel, Wes Morgan, Rihad Mahrez, Andy King and Jeffrey Schlupp all helped win both titles and are proper legends with Foxes fans for their long service and success!

POWER-PACKED STADIUM

The King Power Stadium became Leicester City's new home in 2002. It replaced their Filbert Street ground, which was built in the 1890s. The new stadium has seen some epic action right from the very first season when Leicester City won promotion to the Premier League. The King Power also saw The Foxes win League 1 in 2009 and the Championship in 2014. Perhaps the greatest game at the stadium was when Leicester City came back from 3–1 down to beat Manchester United 5–3 in September 2014.

Page 12 Captain Clues
1. Gary Cahill, 2. Vincent Kompany, 3. Phil Jagielka,
4. Antonio Valencia, 5. Mark Noble, 6. Jordan Henderson,
7. Wes Morgan, 8. Simon Francis

Pages 22-23 Hair We Go!
1. A, 2. C, 3. D, 4. I, 5. G, 6. H, 7. A, 8. B, 9. F

Page 32 Spot the Stars

Page 46 Get to the Ground!
A.Pittodrie Stadium, B.Ibrox Stadium, B.Celtic Park,
D.Easter Road

Page 54 Missing Letters
1. ERIKSEN, 2. MORATA, 3. WILSON

Page 54 Name Game

Page 55 Paying the Penalty   Ball 6.

Page 55 Guess the Year
1. 2016, 2. 2018, 3. 2017

Page 80 Shirt Swap
1. LUKA MILIVOJEVIC, 2. GERARD DEULOFEU,
3. MARKO ARNAUTOVIC, 4. STEVEN DEFOUR,
5. NATHAN AKE, 6. SHINJI OKAZAKI

Pages 88-89 Changing Room Changes